The Real Story of the Superheroes

© Photography and texts
Dulce Pinzón

Creative Director
Ramón Reverté

Publication Coordinator
Isabel Garcés

Design
David Kimura + Gabriela Varela

Translation
Dulce Pinzón

Copy editing
María Teresa González

Prepress
Emilio Breton

c/ Loreto, 13-15 Local B
08029 Barcelona
España

Río Pánuco 141. Col. Cuauhtémoc.
06500 México D.F.
México

info@editorialrm.com
www.editorialrm.com

First edition

Editorial RM, S.A. de C.V. (English): 978-607-7515-81-4
Editorial RM, S.A. de C.V. (Español): 978-607-7515-80-7

RM Verlag (English): 978-84-15118-24-4
RM Verlag (Español): 978-84-15118-23-7

Printed in China
Toppan Printing Co. (C.Z) Ltd.
April 2010

149

This book has been pubished with the support
of the Fondo Nacional para la Cultura y las Artes
through the Programa de Fomento a Proyectos
y Coinversiones Culturales (twenty-seventh
implementation, 2011).

Dulce Pinzón

The Real Story of the Superheroes

Editorial RM

Bernabe Mendez from the state of Guerrero works as a professional window washer in New York. He sends home 500 dollars a month.

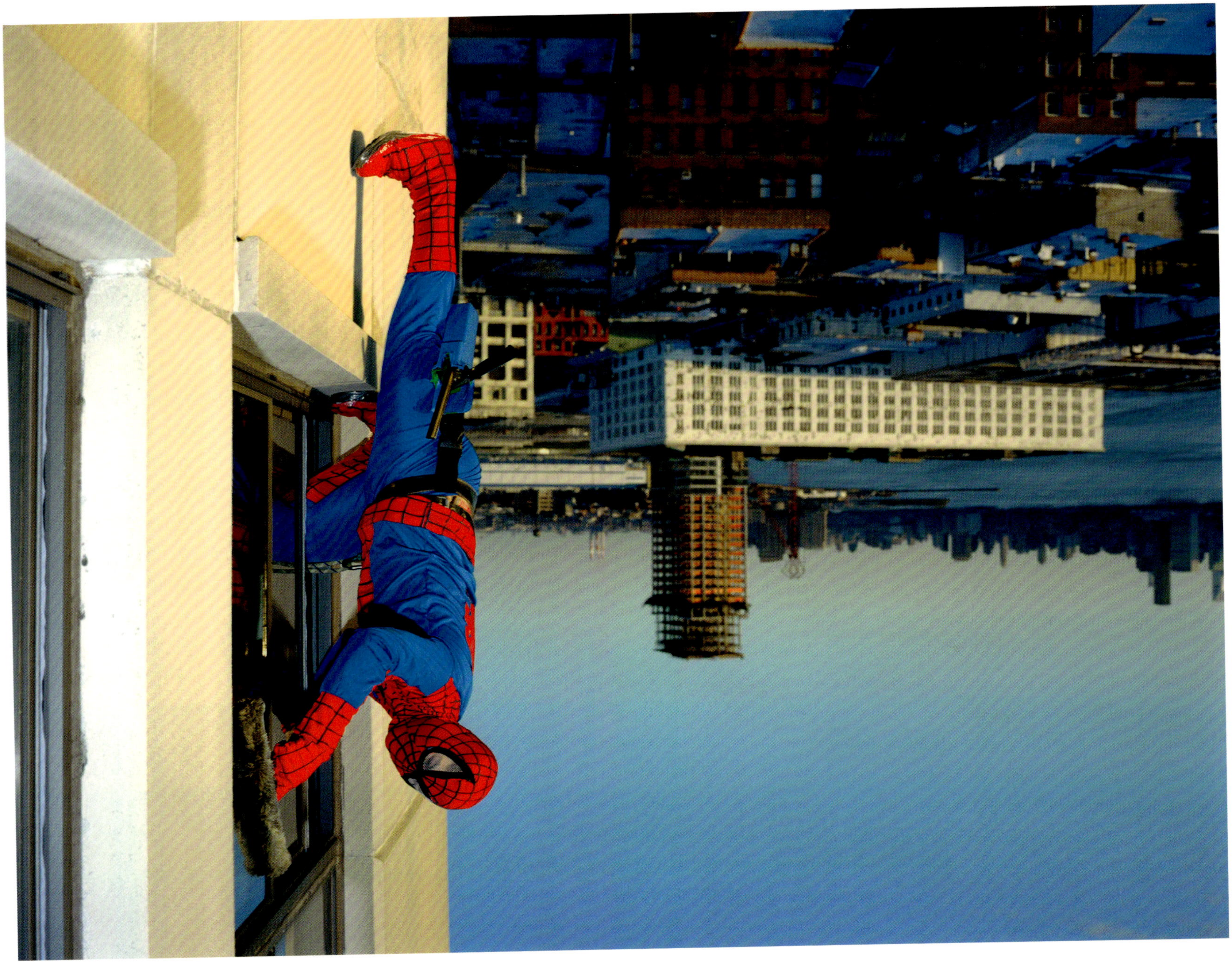

Federico Martinez from the state of Puebla works as a taxi driver in New York. He sends home 250 dollars a week.

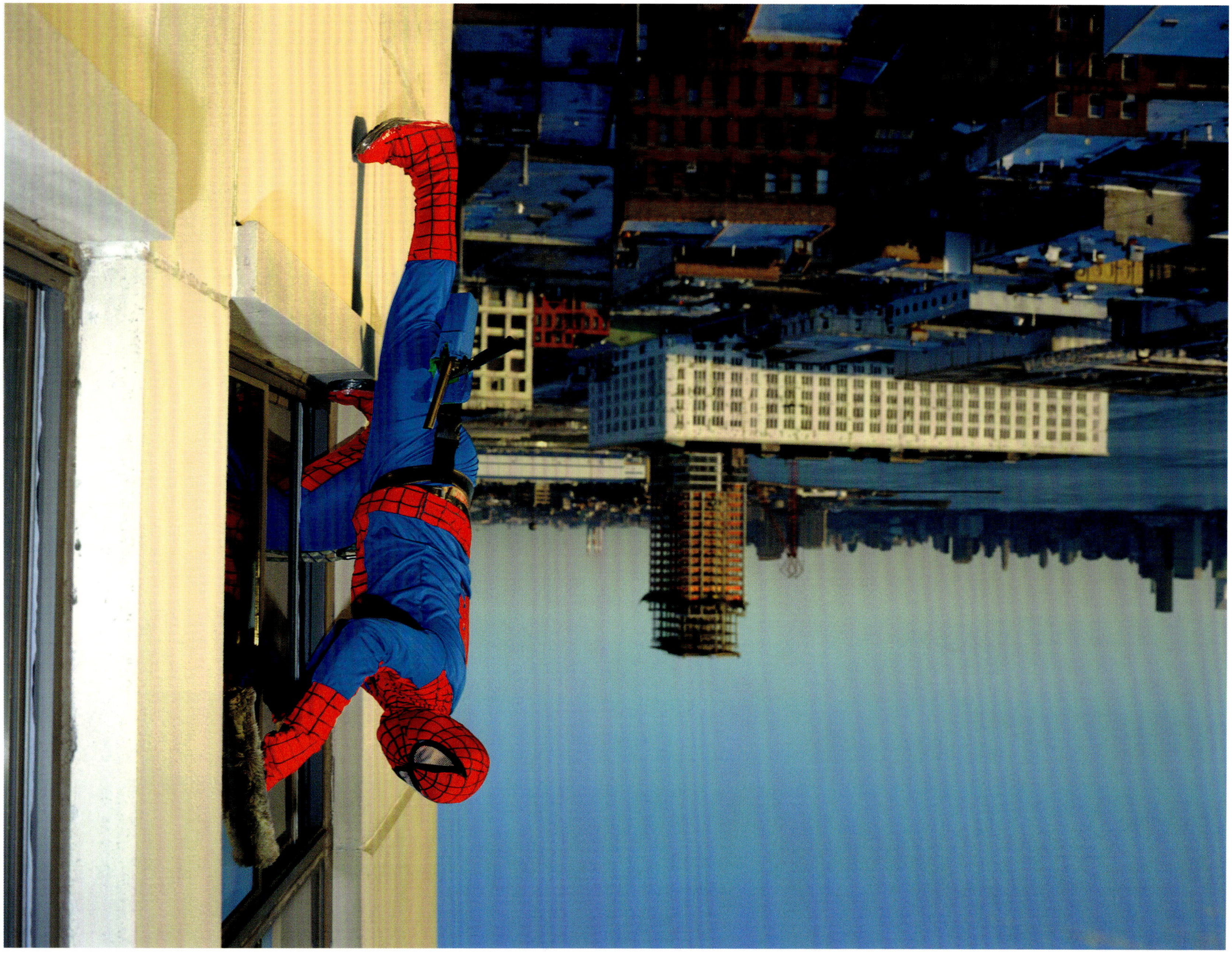

Minerva Valencia from Puebla works as a nanny in New York. She sends home 400 dollars a week.

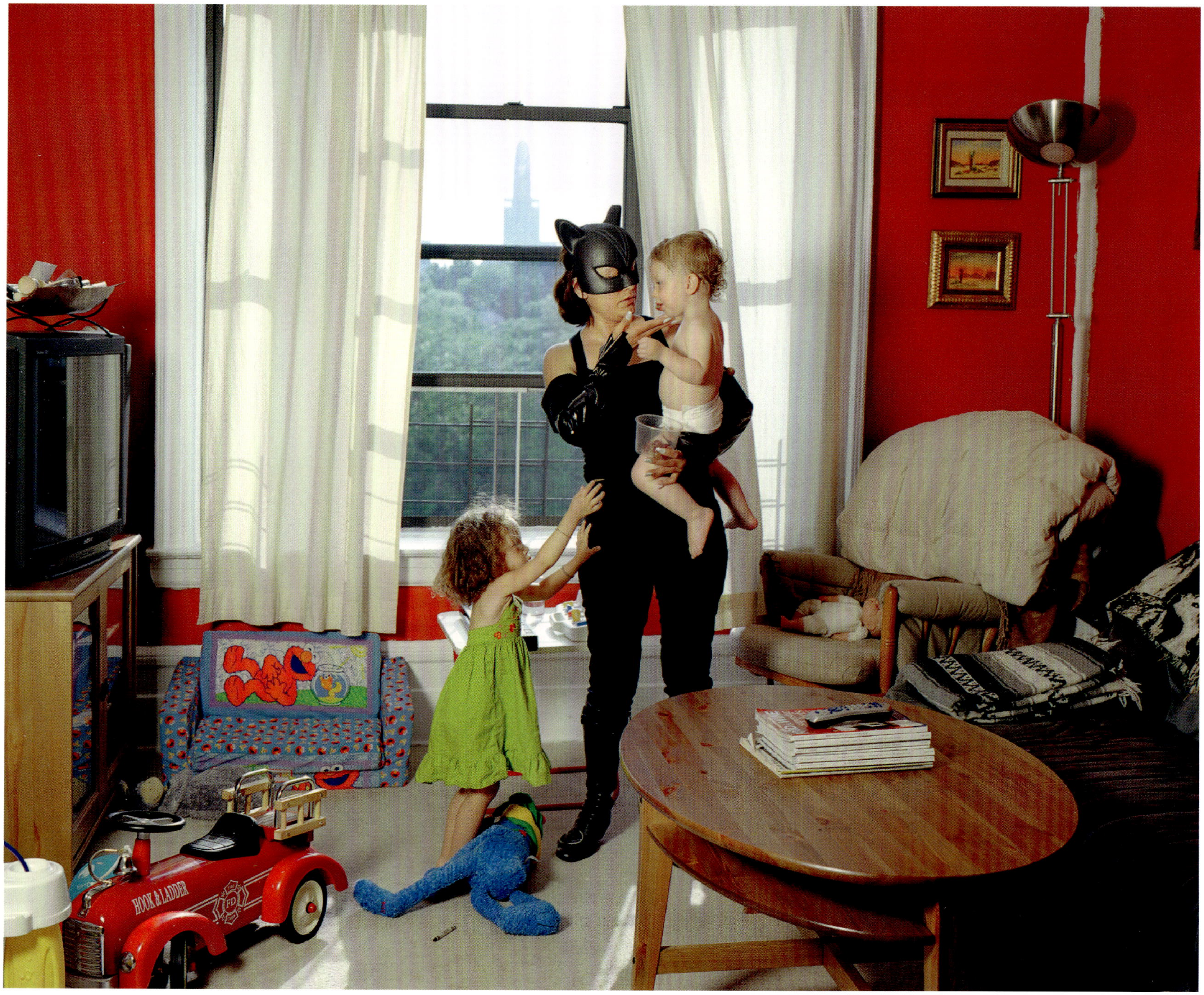
HOOK & LADDER

Federico Martinez from the state of Puebla works as a taxi driver in New York. He sends home 250 dollars a week.

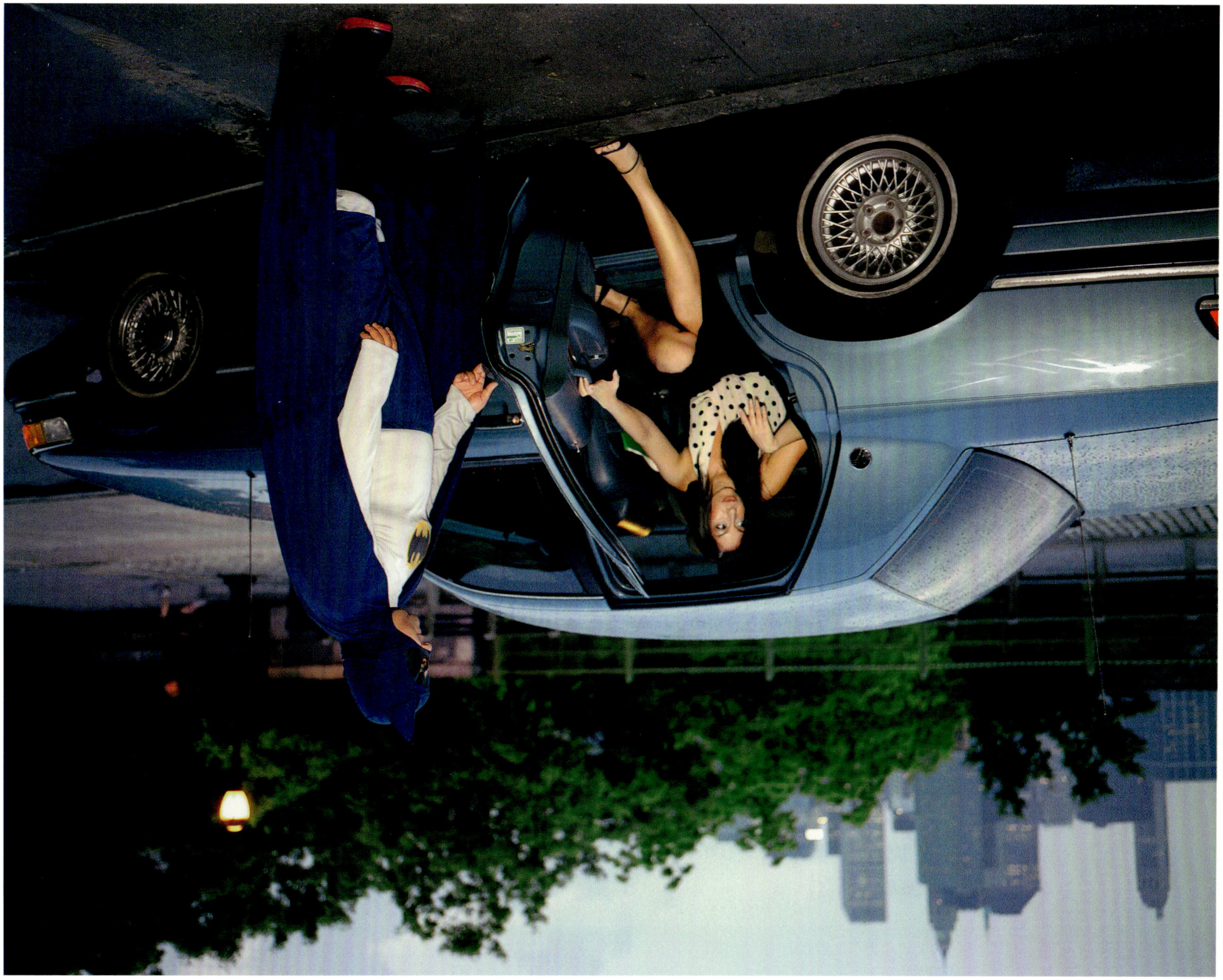

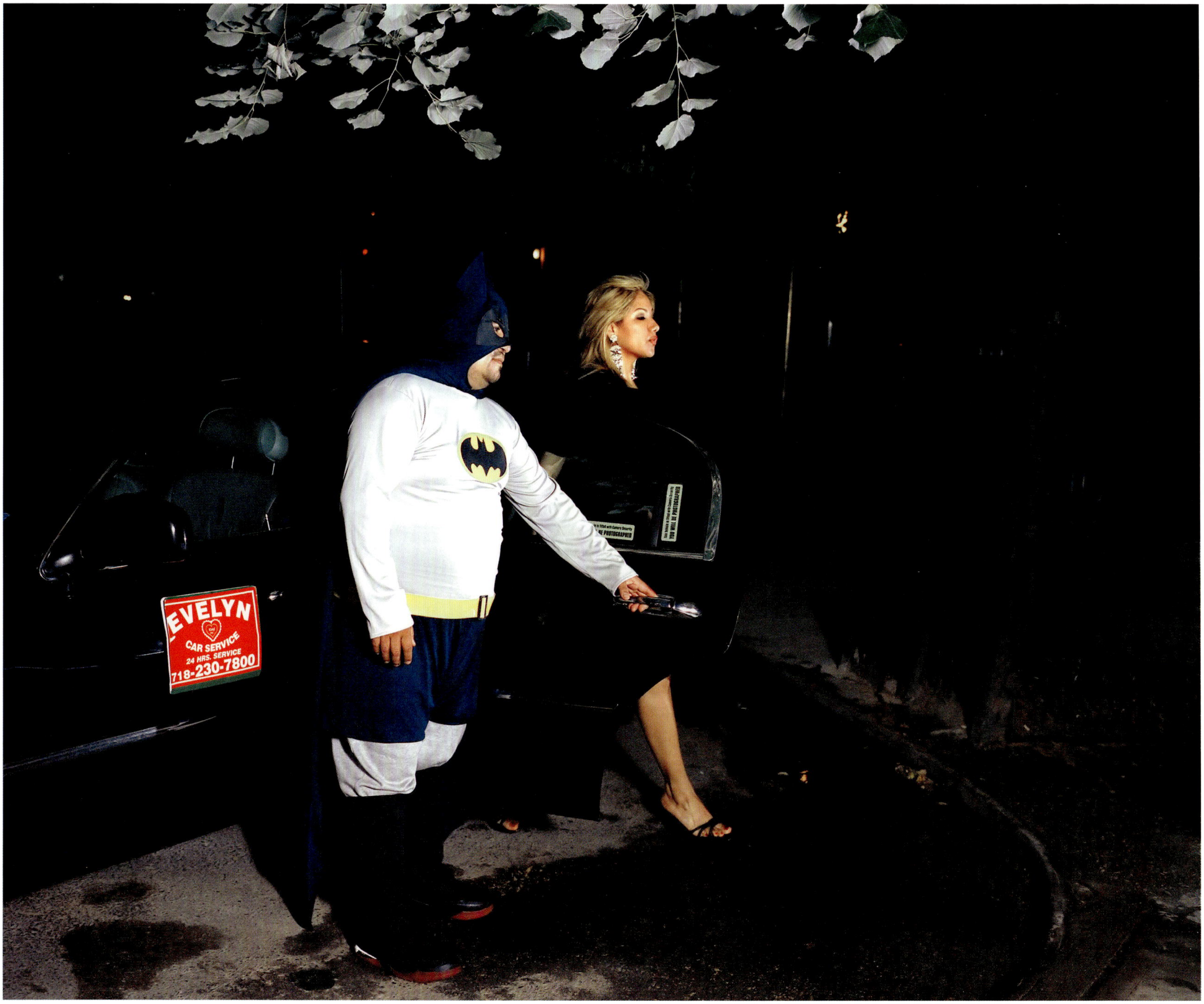
EVELYN
CAR SERVICE
24 HRS. SERVICE
718-230-7800

Ernesto Mendez from Mexico City works as a gigolo in Times Square, New York. He sends home 200 dollars a week.

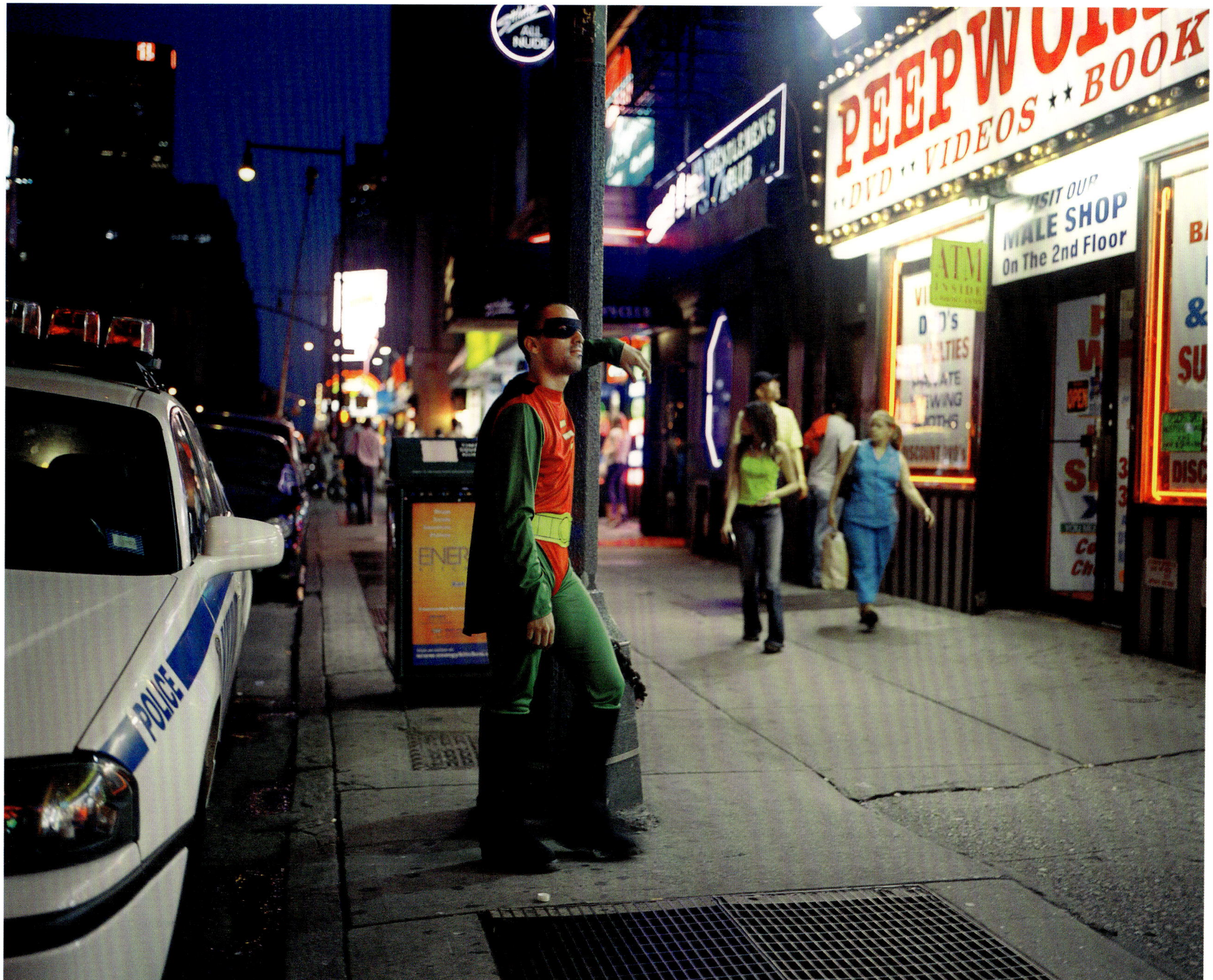
ALL NUDE
DVD VIDEOS
VISIT OUR
MALE SHOP
On The 2nd Floor
ATM
INSIDE
POLICE

Roman Romero from Tlapa, Guerrero works as a superintendent in New York. He sends home 800 dollars a month.

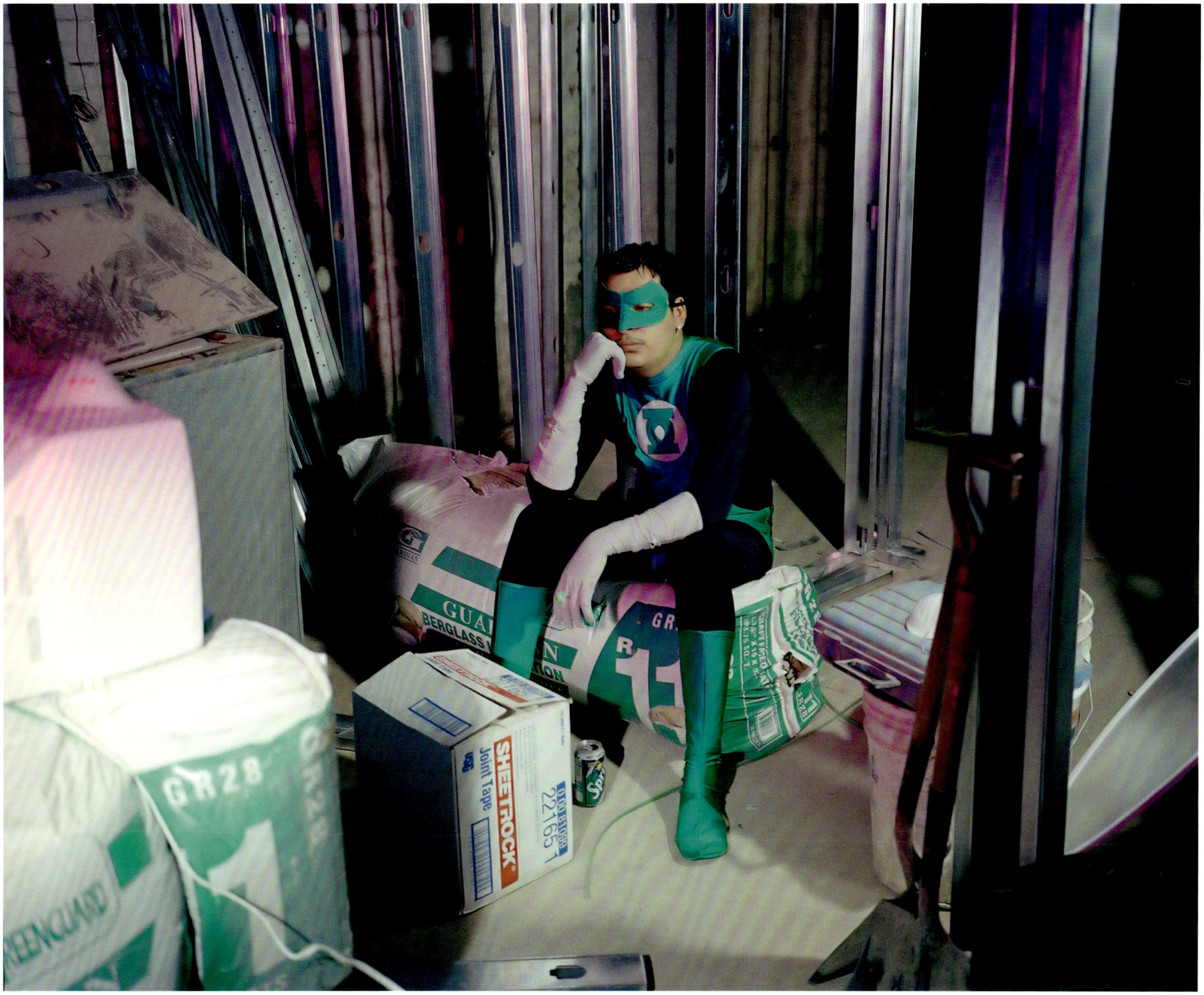
GR28
SHEETROCK
Joint Tape
221651

Adalberto Lara from state of Mexico works as a construction worker in New York. He sends home 350 dollars a week.

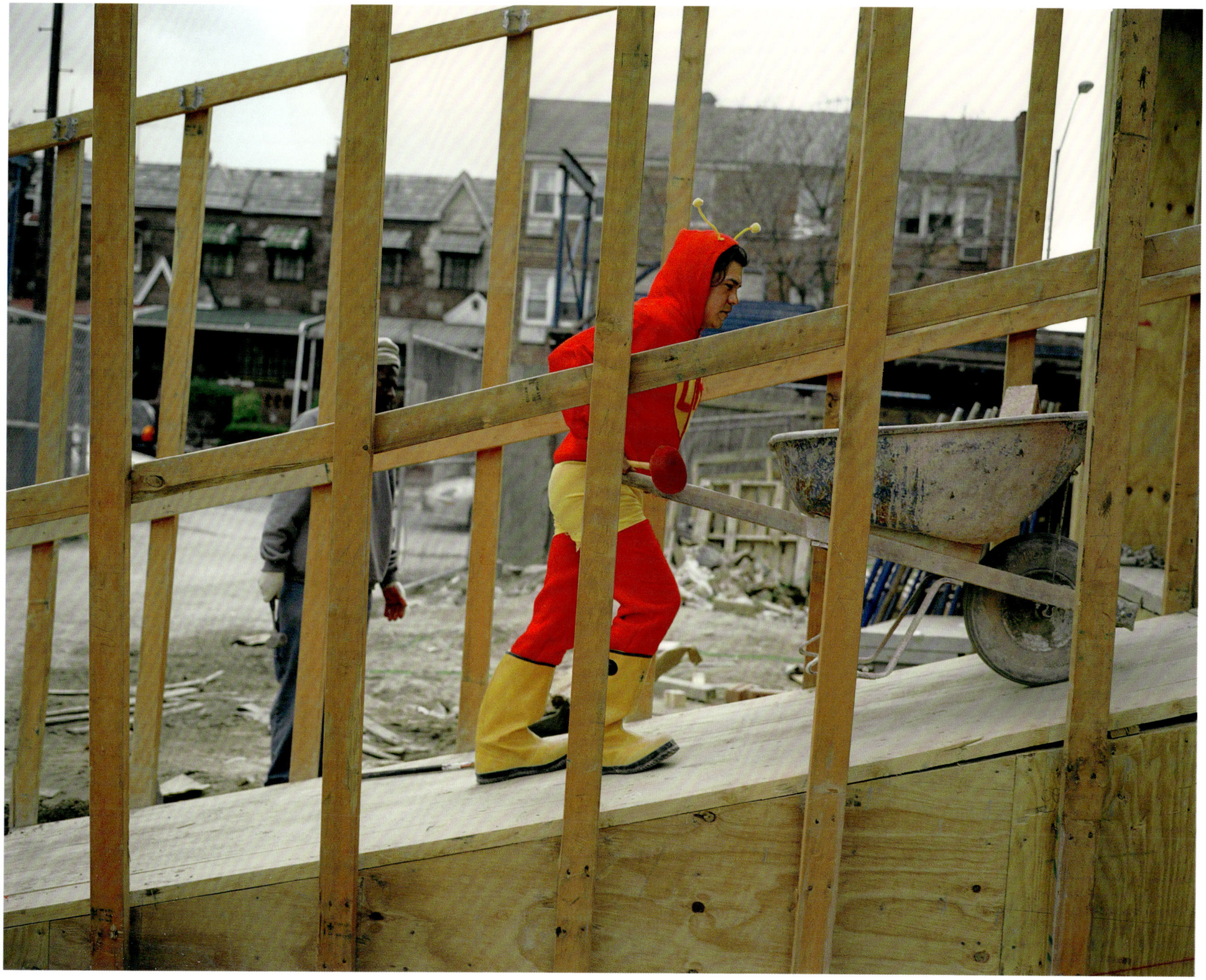

Paulino Cardozo from the state of Guerrero works unloading trucks at a greengrocer's. He sends home 300 dollars a week.

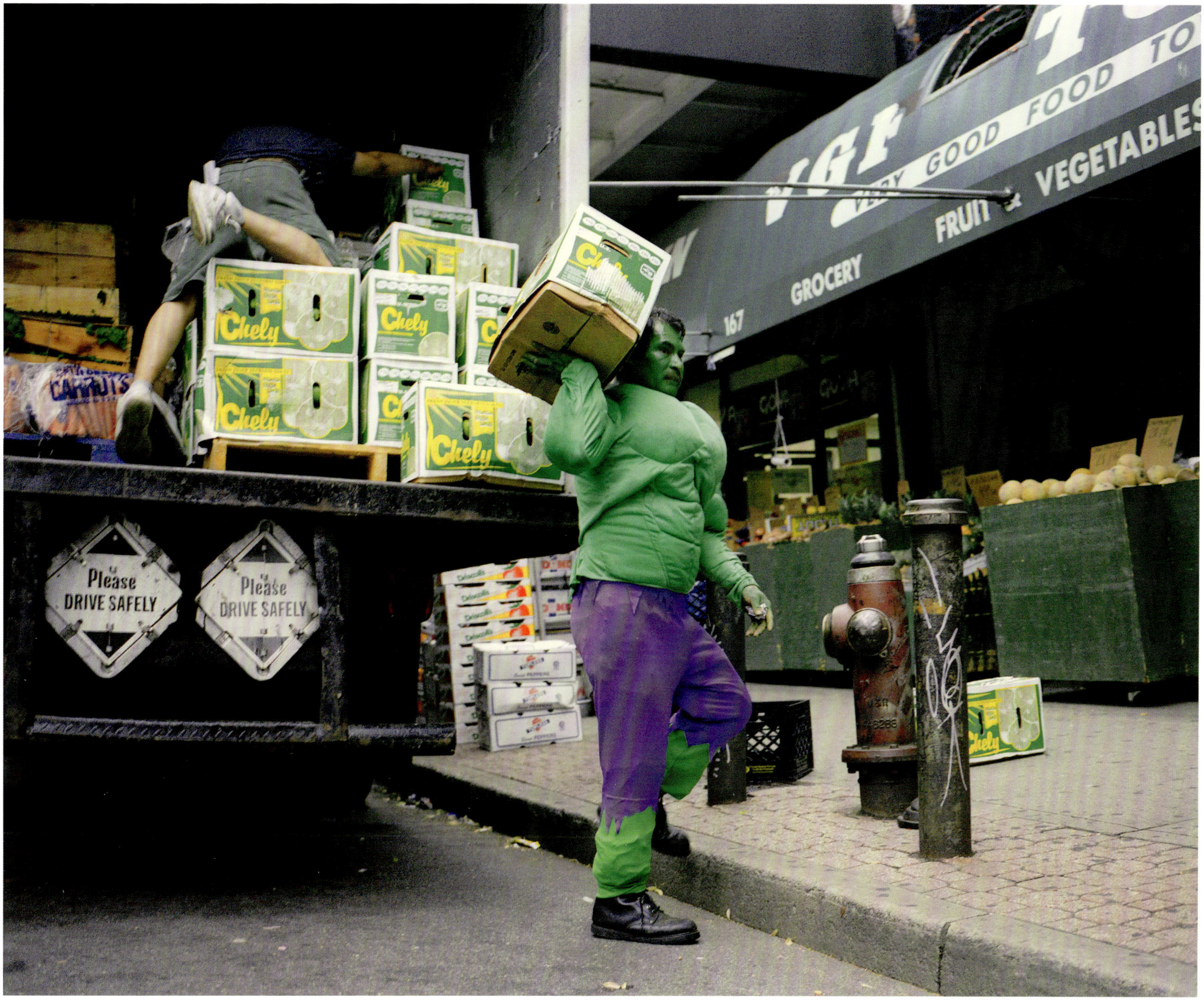
VERY GOOD FOOD TO
FRUIT & VEGETABLES
GROCERY
167
Chely
CARROTS
Please
DRIVE SAFELY
Please
DRIVE SAFELY

Juventino Rosas from state of Mexico works in a fish market in New York. He sends home 400 dollars a week.

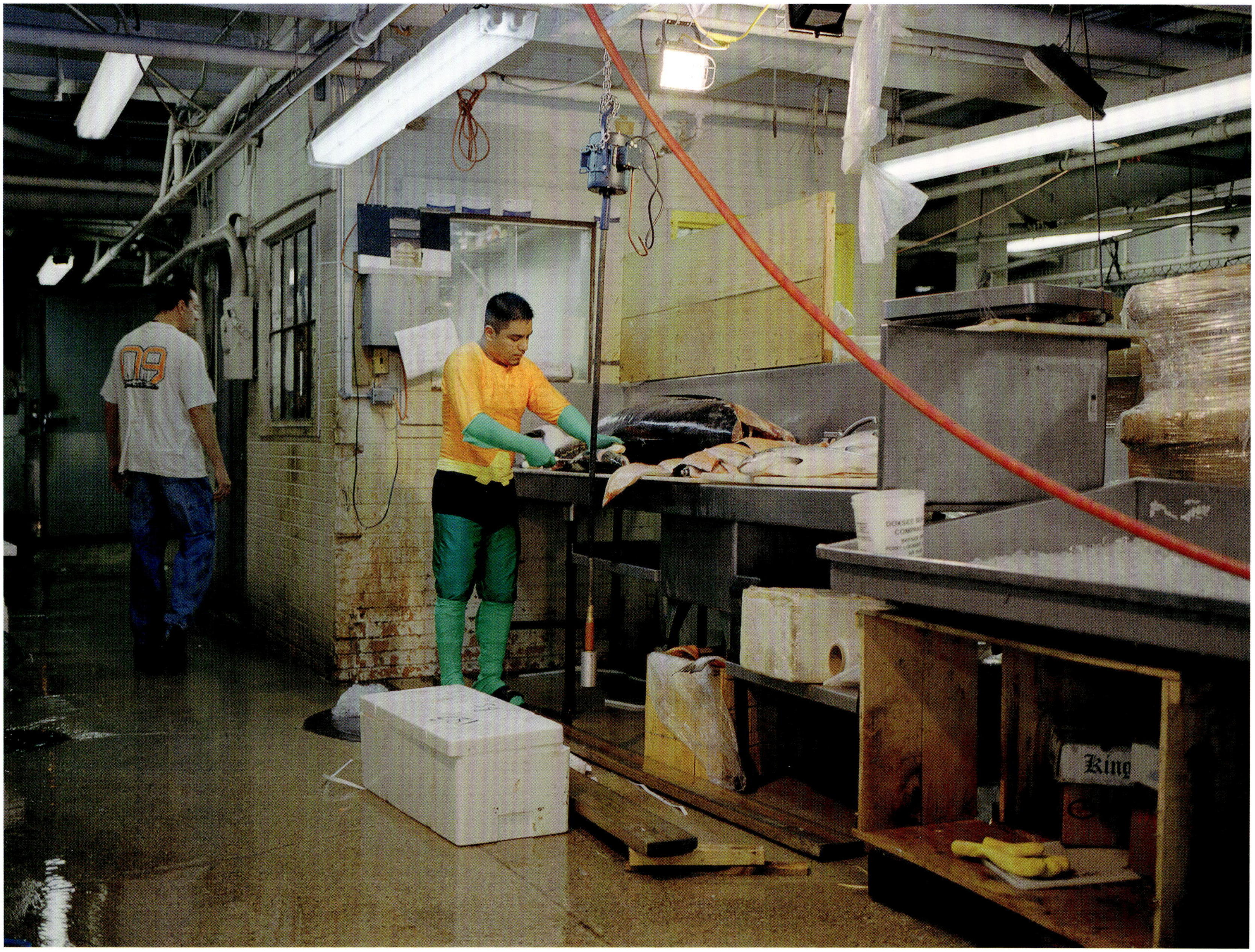
King

Sergio Garcia from state of Mexico works as a waiter in New York. He sends home 350 dollars a week.

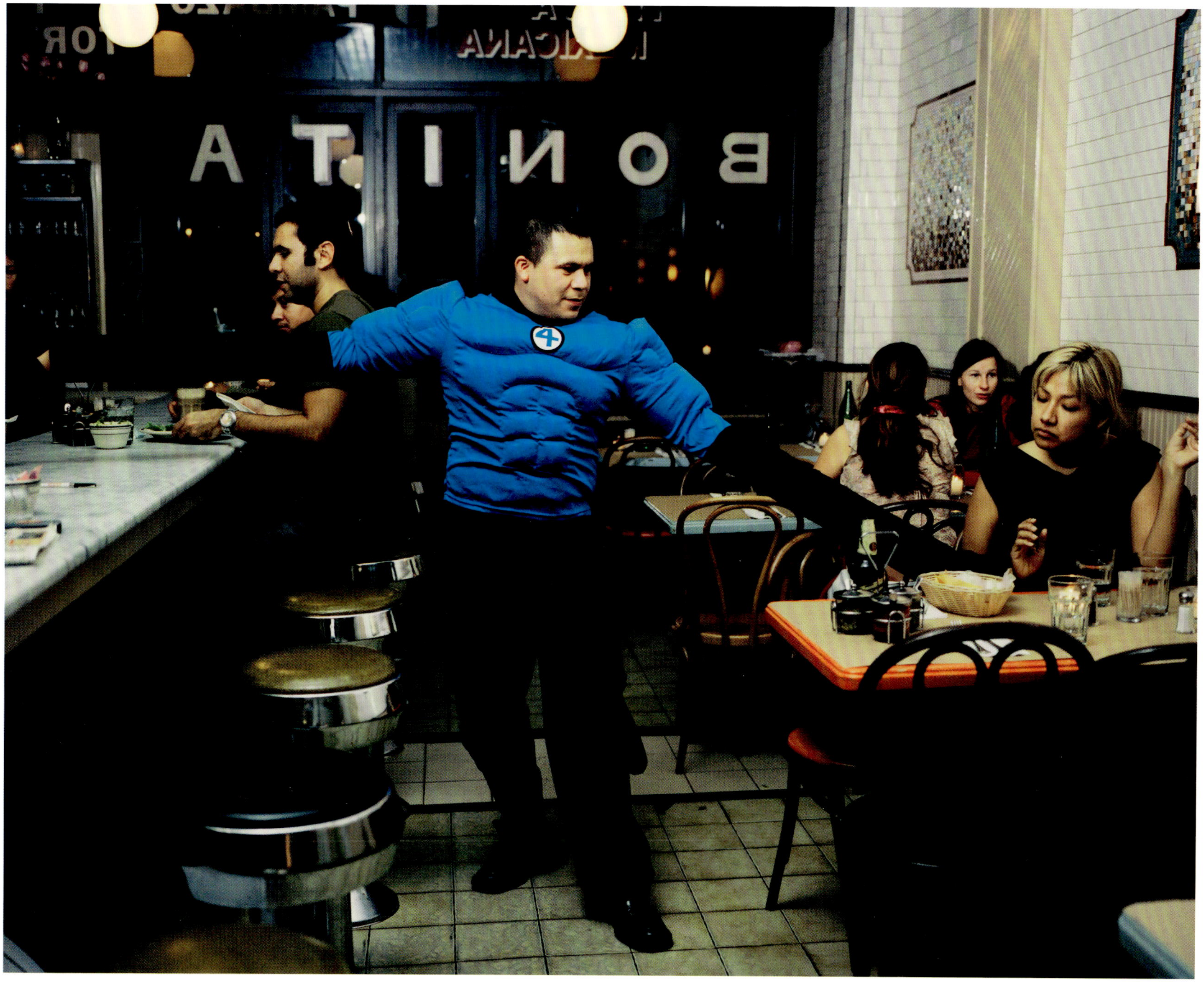

Oscar Gonzalez from the state of Oaxaca works as a cook in New York. He sends home 350 dollars a week.

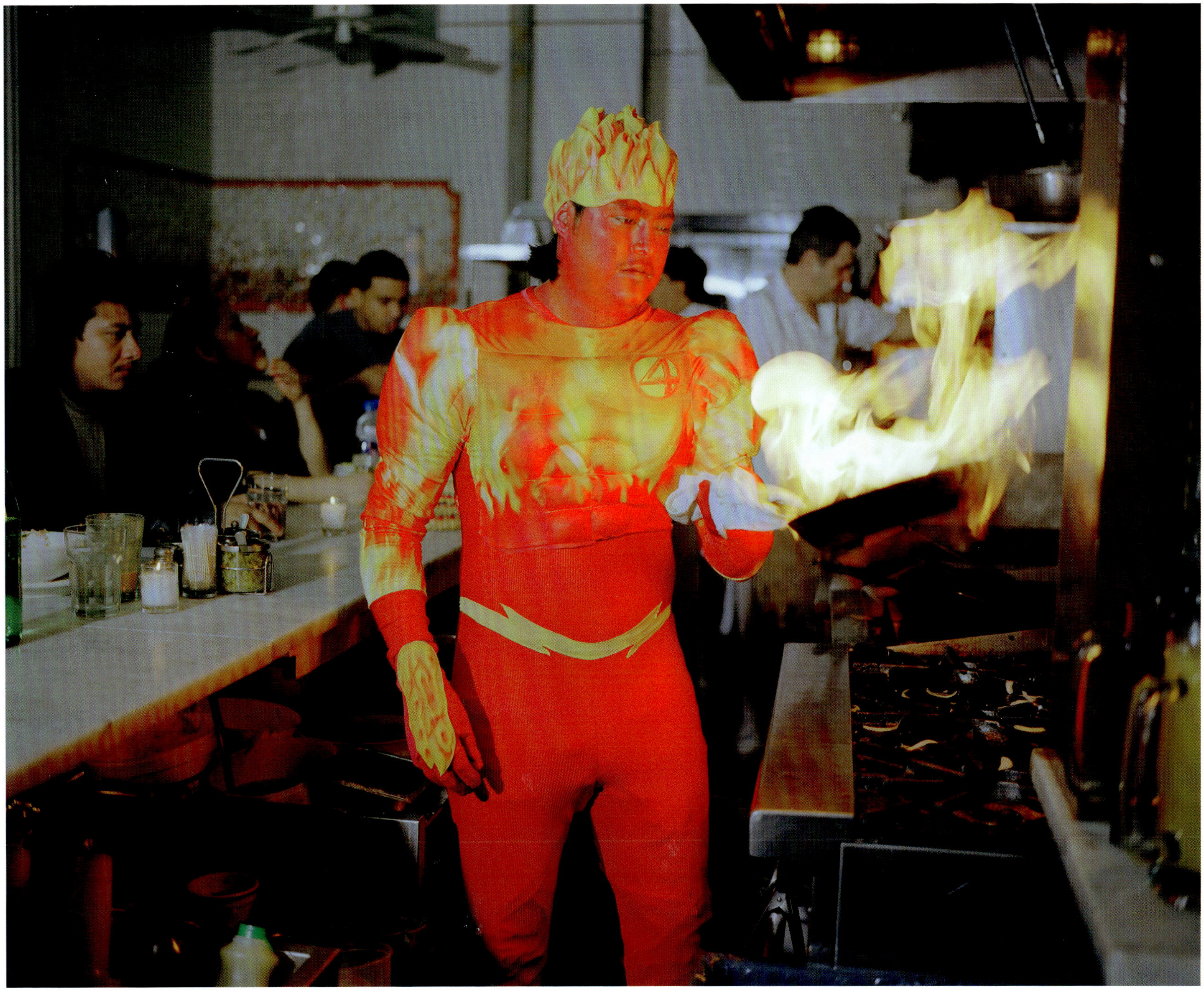

Elizabeth and **Enrique Alonso** from the state of Puebla work in a restaurant in New York. They send home 400 dollars a week.

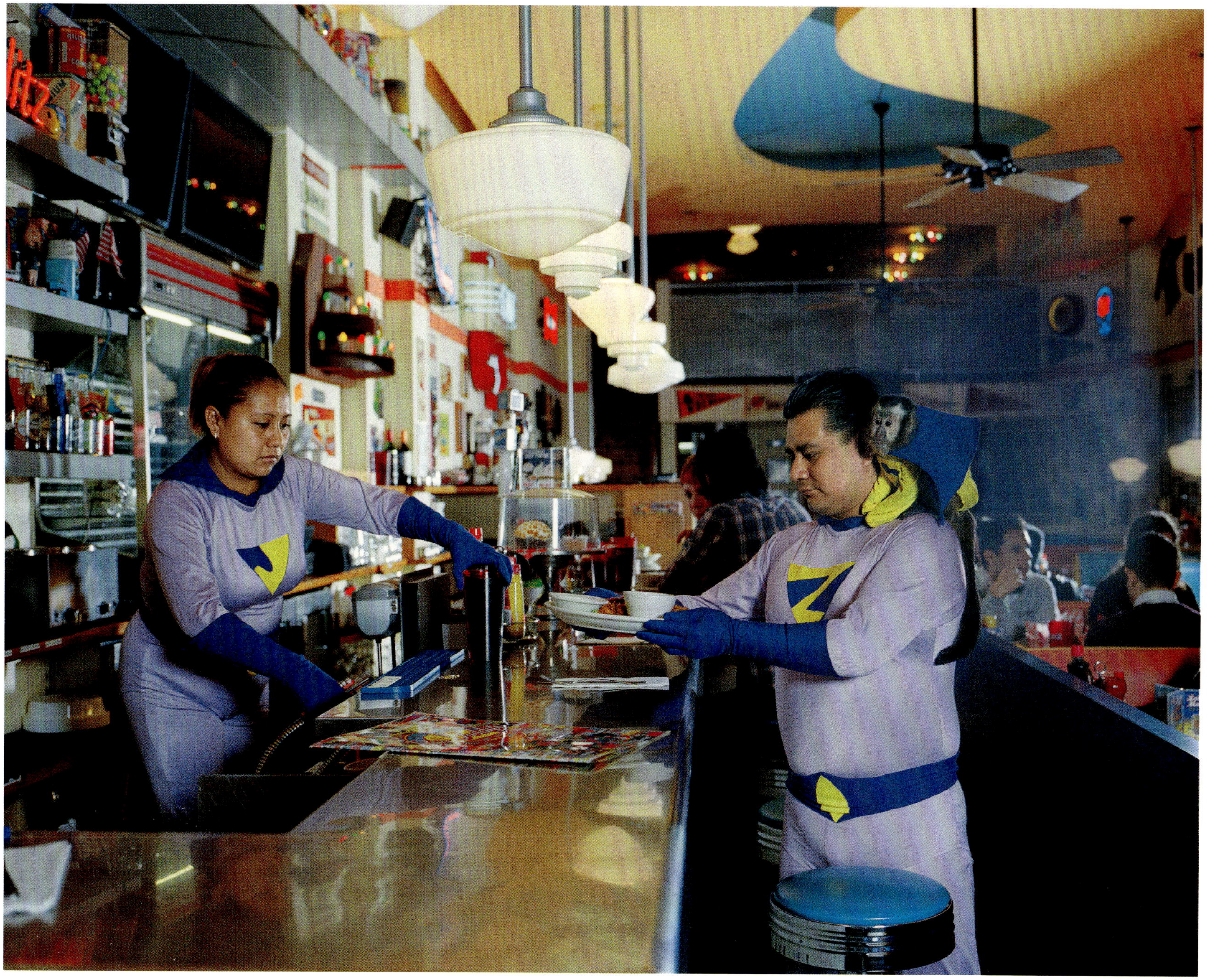

Bolivar Abril from Quito, Ecuador works as an ice cream man in New York. He sends home 250 dollars a week.

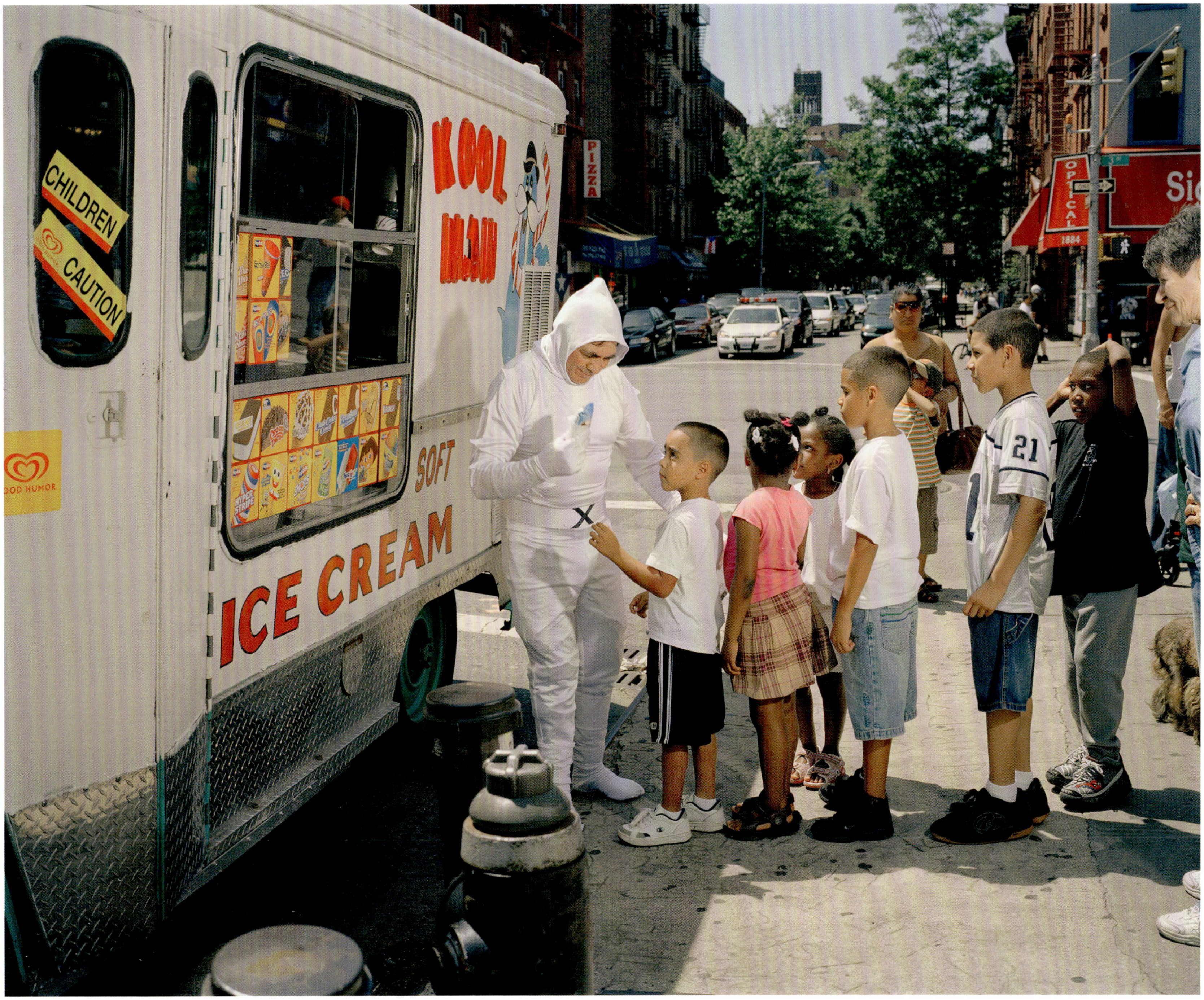
CHILDREN
CAUTION
KOOL MAN
SOFT
ICE CREAM
PIZZA
OPTICAL

Jose Rosendo de Jesus from the state of Guerrero works as a union organizer in New York. He sends home 700 a month.

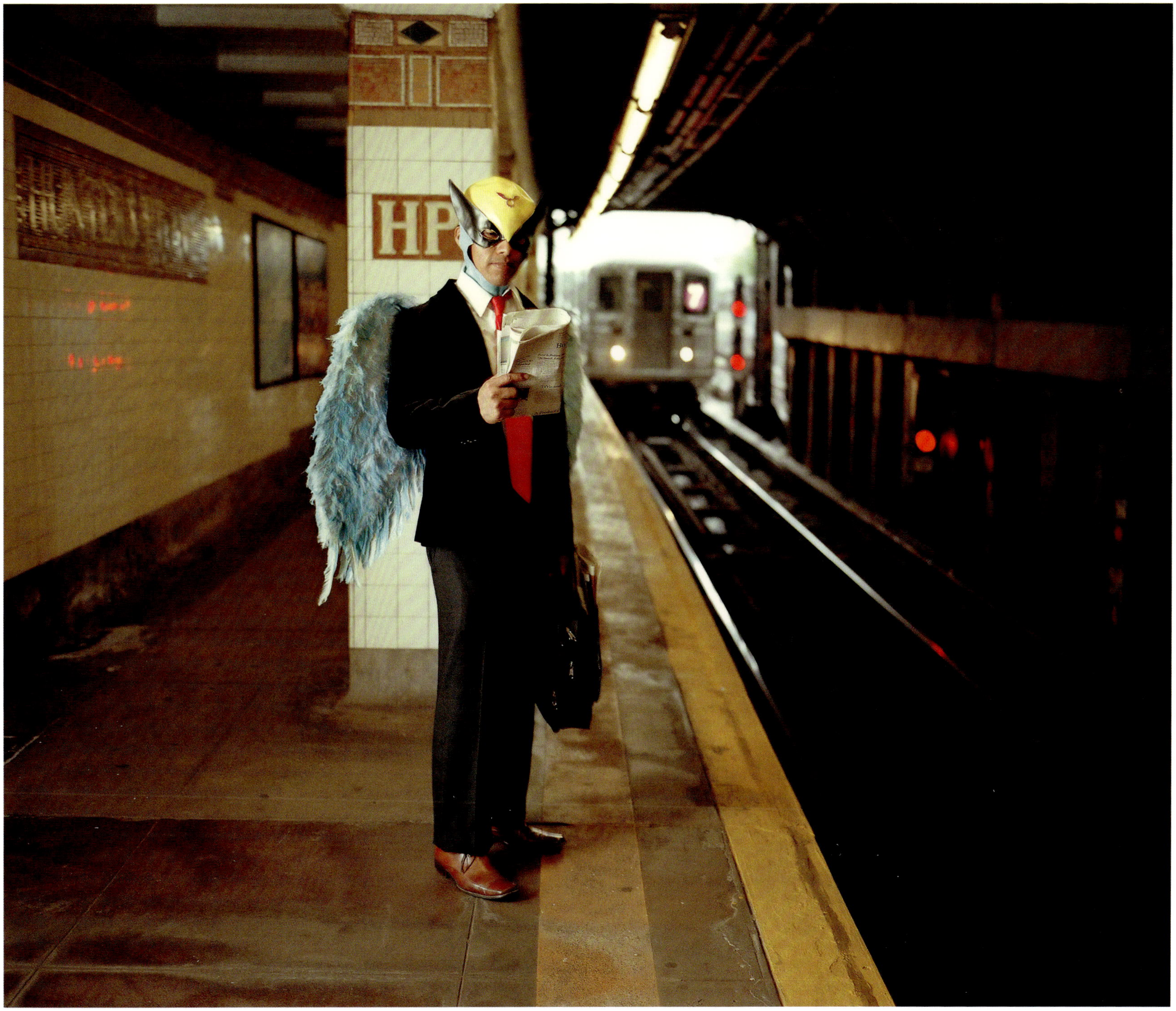
HP

Roy Acosta from Puerto Rico works as a policeman in New York. He sends home 300 dollars a week.

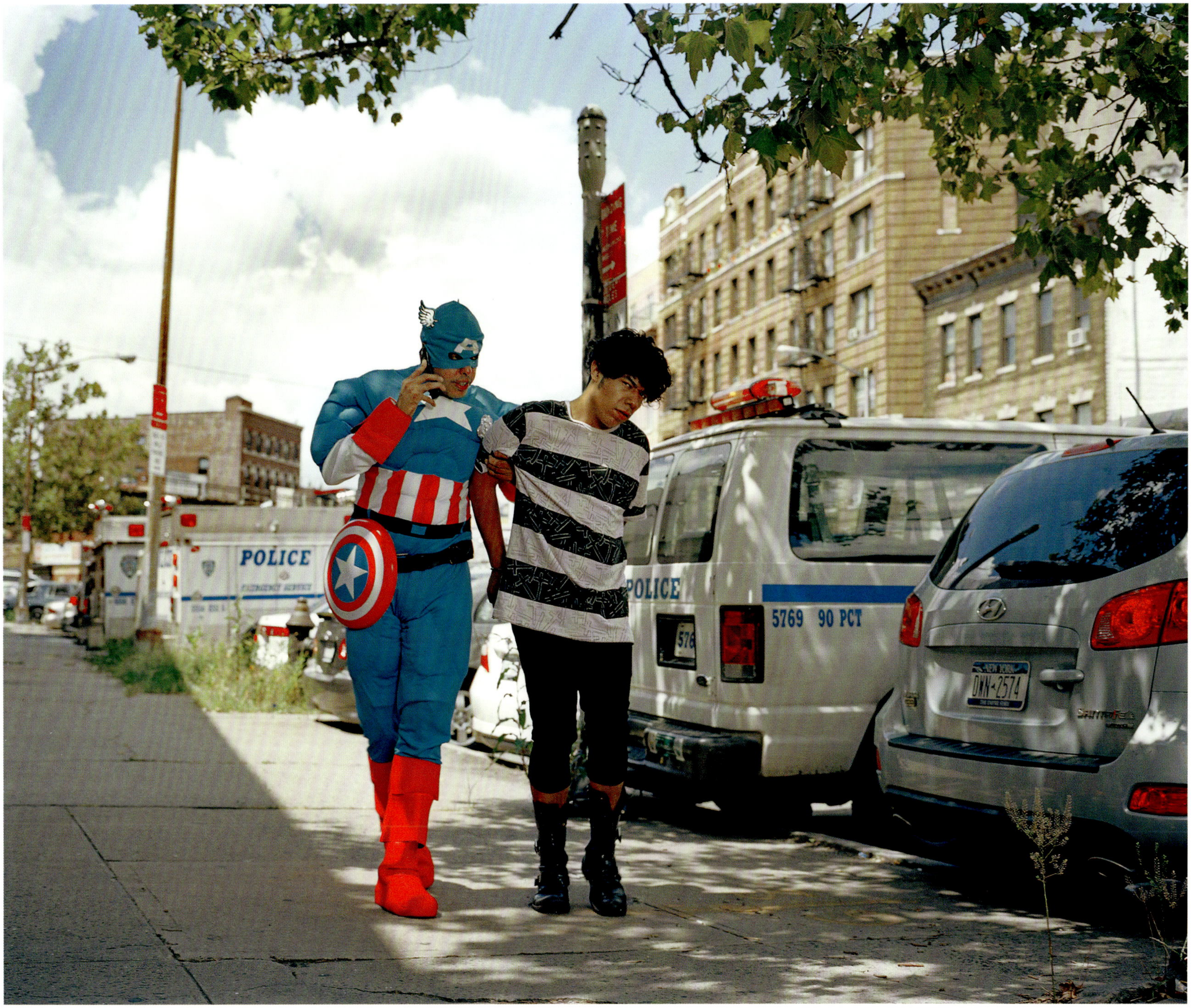
POLICE
POLICE
5769 90 PCT

Alvaro Cruz from state of Mexico works as a cook and runs with *Los Compadres*. He sends home 300 dollars a month.

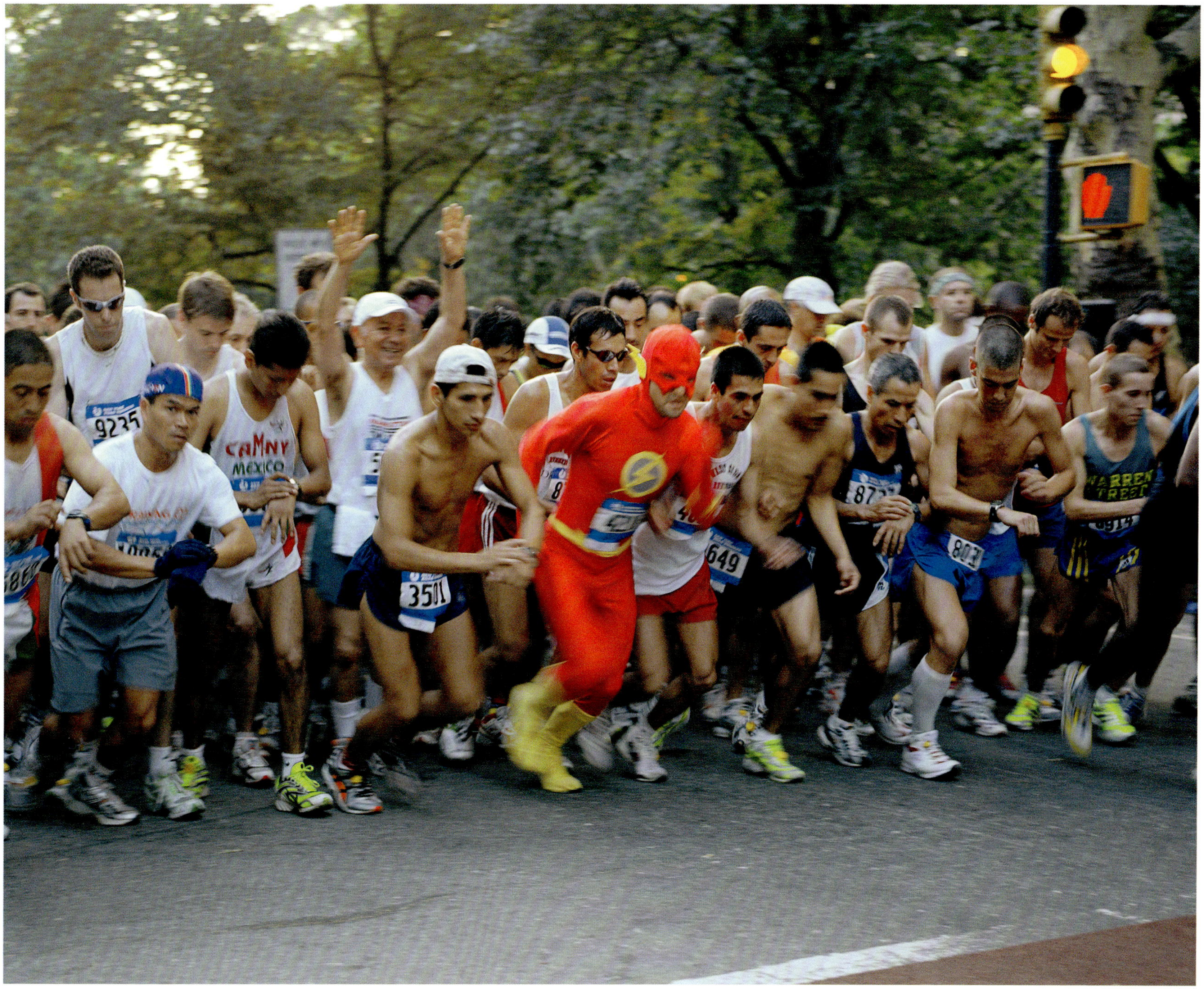
9235
CAMNY
MEXICO
3501
WARREN

Maria Luisa Romero from the state of Puebla works in a laundromat in Brooklyn, New York. She sends home 150 dollars a week.

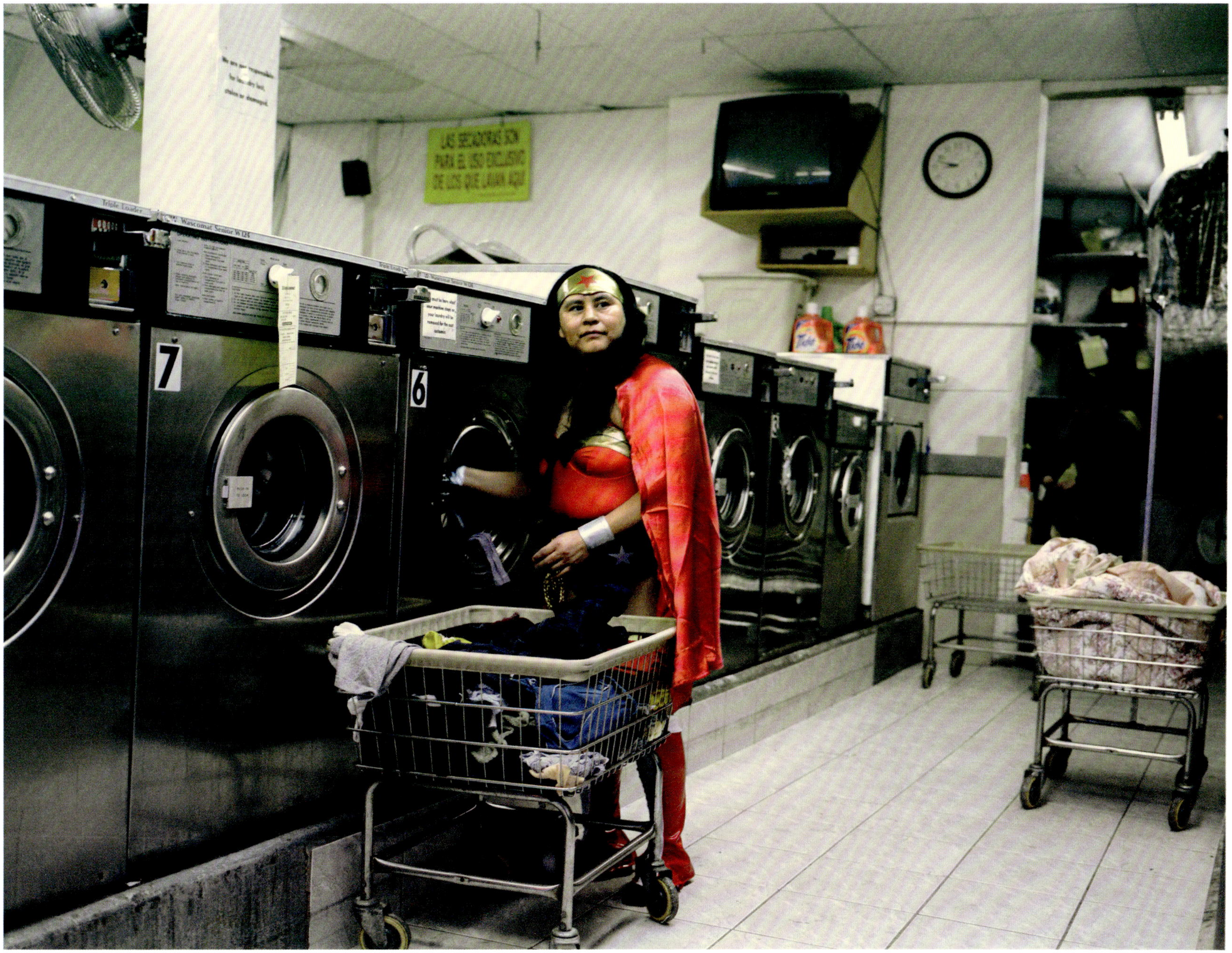
LAS SECADORAS SON
PARA EL USO EXCLUSIVO
DE LOS QUE LAVAN AQUI
7
6

Noe Reyes from the state of Puebla works as a delivery man in Brooklyn, New York. He sends home 500 dollars a week.

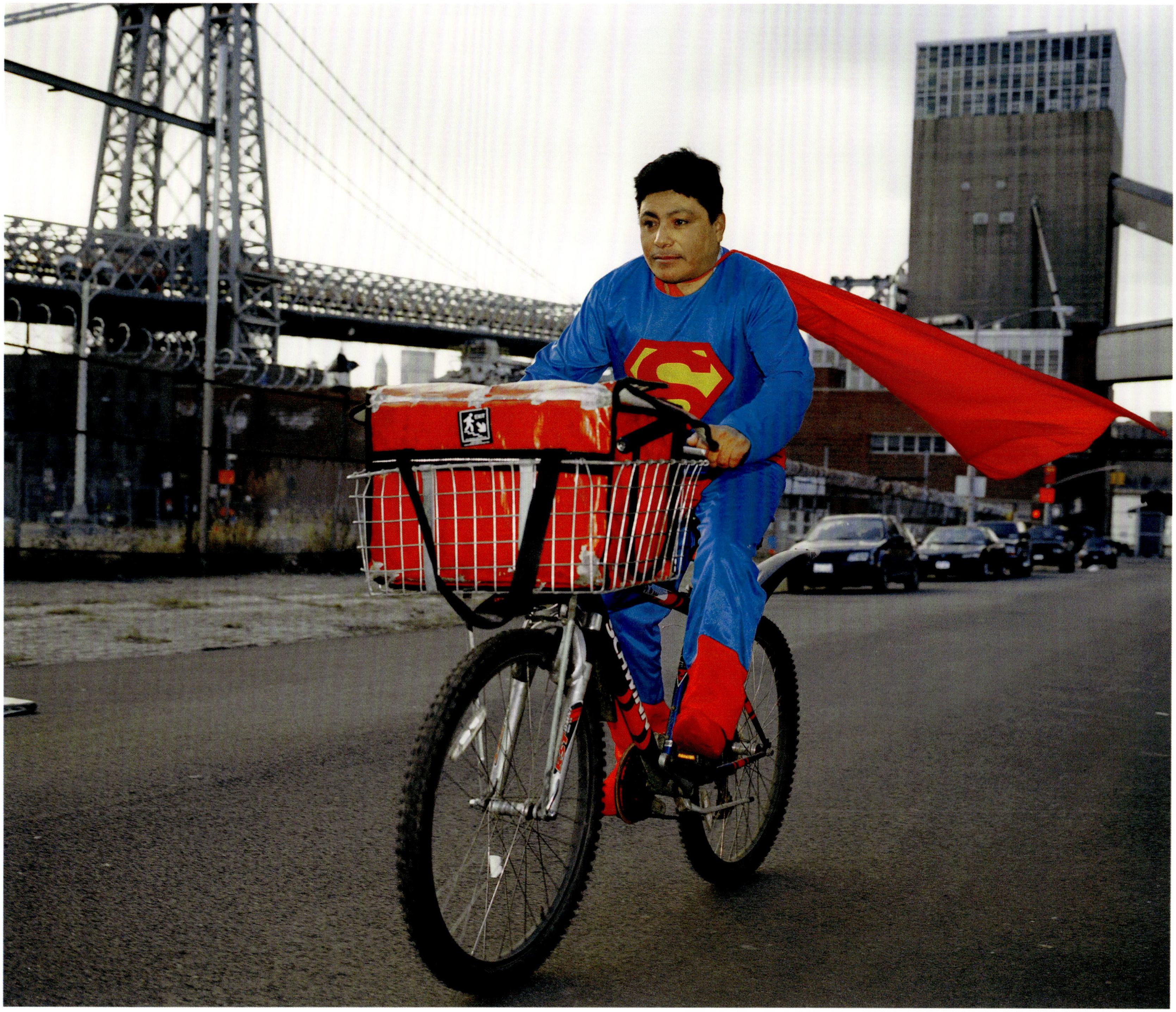

Dulce Pinzón from México City works as a photographer and would like to pay tribute to all the wonderful people who collaborated with her to make this project possible.

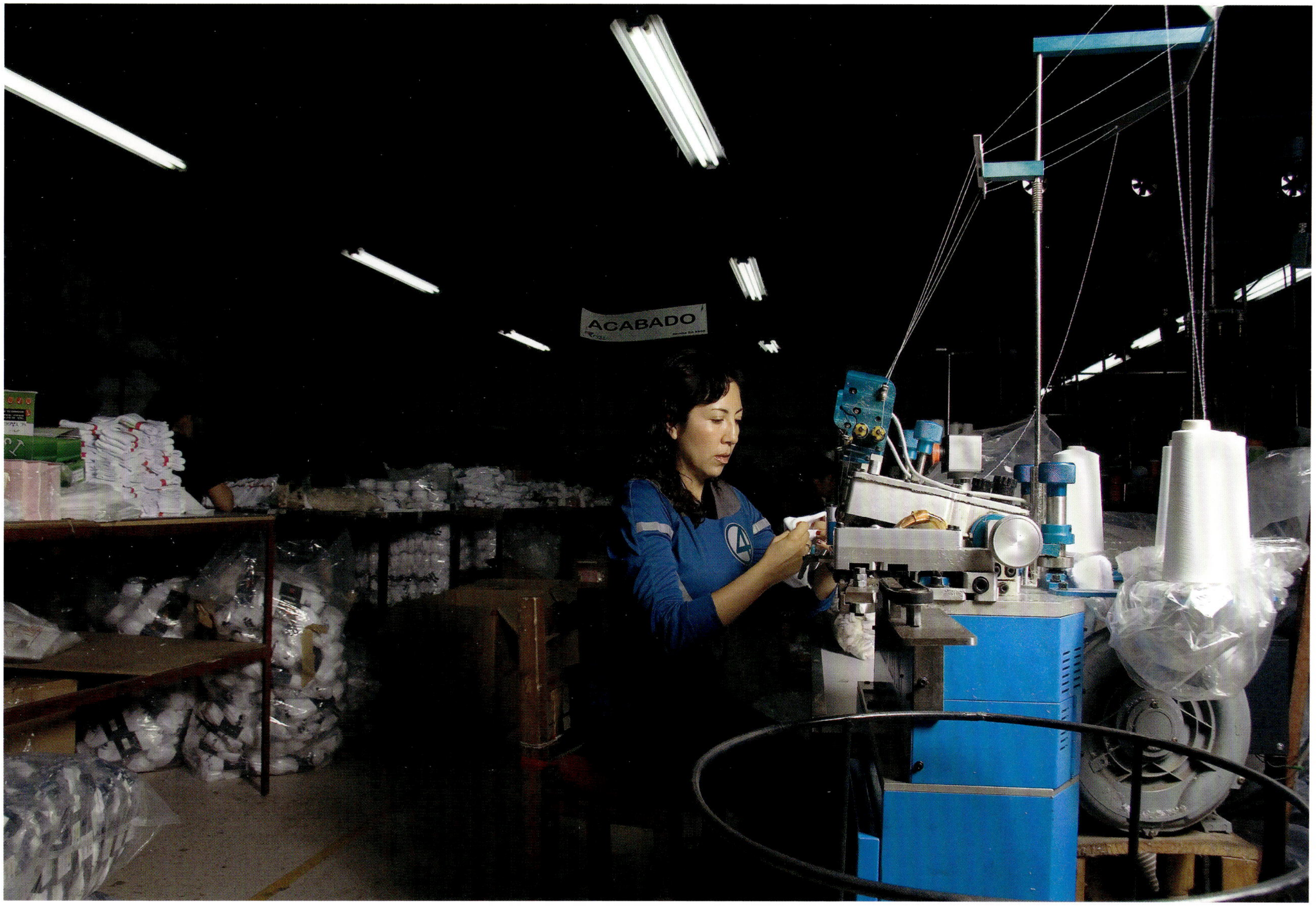
ACABADO

The Real Story of the Superheroes

After September 11th, the notion of the "hero" began to rear its head in the public consciousness more and more frequently. The notion served a necessity in a time of national and global crisis to acknowledge those who showed extraordinary courage or determination in the face of danger, sometimes even sacrificing their lives in an attempt to save others. However, in the whirlwind of journalism surrounding these deservedly front-page disasters and emergencies, it is easy to take for granted the heroes who sacrifice immeasurable life and labor in their day to day lives for the good of others, but do so in a somewhat less spectacular setting.

The Mexican immigrant worker in New York is a perfect example of the hero who has gone unnoticed. It is common for a Mexican worker in New York to work extraordinary hours in extreme conditions for very low wages which are saved at great cost and sacrifice and sent to families and communities in Mexico who rely on them to survive.

The Mexican economy has quietly become dependent on the money sent from workers in the United States. Conversely, the US economy has quietly become dependent on the labor of Mexican immigrants. Along with the depth of their sacrifice, it is the quietness of this dependence which makes Mexican immigrant workers a subject of interest.

The principal objective of this series is to pay homage to these brave and determined men and women that somehow manage, without the help of any supernatural power, to withstand extreme conditions of labor in order to help their families and communities survive and prosper.

This project consists of twenty color photographs of Mexican and Latino immigrants dressed in the costumes of popular American and Mexican superheroes. Each photo pictures the worker/superhero in their work environment, and is accompanied by a short text including the worker's name, their hometown, and the amount of money they send to their families each week.

La verdadera historia de los Superhéroes

A partir del 11 de Septiembre de 2001 la noción de héroe resurgió en gran medida impulsada por la necesidad de reconocer la labor de las personas que sacrificaron su vida o que de manera extraordinaria enfrentaron con valor situaciones de peligro. Sin embargo, es importante fijar estos valores no sólo en la persona que emerge como héroe debido a una desgracia o una emergencia nacional o mundial, sino en aquella que día a día sacrifica parte de su vida con el fin de mejorar su realidad y afectar positivamente la de los otros.

En el contexto de la cultura pop, un superhéroe exige que un determinado personaje posea poderes extra humanos para salvar y proteger a sus congéneres. Traducido a la vida cotidiana, un poder extraordinario puede ser, por ejemplo, la capacidad de sobrevivir en condiciones extremas —ya sea laborales o climáticas—, sacrificar hasta la vida para ayudar a los seres queridos, o materializar los sueños de aquellos que lo esperan en casa.

Siguiendo esta idea, el libro *La verdadera historia de los Superhéroes* muestra una serie de 20 fotografías a color de inmigrantes mexicanos y latinoamericanos que desde los Estados Unidos, en particular desde la ciudad de Nueva York, apoyan a sus comunidades y representan una fuerza significativa en el desarrollo económico de sus países de origen y de la nación americana. Los inmigrantes, vestidos como los superhéroes de la cultura popular estadounidense y mexicana, aparecen retratados en su ambiente laboral. Cada imagen se acompaña de un breve texto que incluye el nombre de la persona y de la comunidad de donde proviene, así como la cantidad de dinero que envía a su familia semanalmente. El principal objetivo es rendir homenaje al hombre ordinario que, carente de poder supernatural, logra que su comunidad sobreviva y progrese.

For Mariano

Dedicated to:
My parents and Moisés

Special acknowledgments:

Adalberto Lara
Alvaro Cruz
Bernabe Mendez
Bolivar Abril
Elizabeth Alonso
Enrique Alonso
Erick Montes
Federico Martinez
Juventino Rosas
Luis Hernandez
Maria Luisa Romero
Minerva Valencia
Noe Reyes
Oscar Gonzalez
Paulino Cardozo
Roman Romero
Jose Rosendo de Jesus
Roy Acosta
Sergio Garcia

Thanks for their help to:

Alan Yee
Aldo Sanchez
Alejandro Almanza
Alejandro Castellanos
Alex Ramos
AJ Jonhson
Amylu Meneses
Ana de Orbegoso
Angelina Mike
Big Daddy's Dinner
Bonitas Restaurant
Carmen Jasso
Cecilia Jurado
César López
Charlotte from Tamed Animals
Denisse Tatemura
Dulce Torres
Erika Harsh
Fernando Almaguer
G. Marquez
Iván Freaner
Juan Carlos Eljure
Julian Johnson
Juliana Hawawini
Julieta Cervantes
Karina Díaz
Kenny Mack
Kool Man Ice Cream
Ludie Stribling
Miguel García
Mr. Sullivan Walsh
Nacho Rincon
NALAC Fund for the Arts, the Ford Foundation, and Southwest Airlines
New York Road Runners Club
Queens Museum of Art
Raúl Zorrilla
Riki Razo
Robert Peguero
Roberto Jimeno
Sandra Mack-Valencia
Tania Jimenez
Teresa Rojas
Tonatiuh Pellizzi
Valeria Treves

The Real Story of the Superheroes
was printed in China in March 2012
by Toppan Printing Co. (C.Z.) Ltd.
It is set in Minion Pro, designed
by Robert Slimbach in 1990. A total
of 2,500 copies were printed on
LumiSilk 150 gsm matt art paper.